MOODS OF THE
SOUTH DOWNS

A PHOTOGRAPHIC JOURNEY FROM
EASTBOURNE TO WINCHESTER

IAIN McGOWAN

HALSGROVE

First published in Great Britain in 2007

Title page photograph: *Late Summer, Bignor Hill*

British Library Cataloguing-in-Publication Data
A CIP record for this title is available from the British Library

ISBN 978 1 84114 595 2

HALSGROVE
Halsgrove House, Ryelands Farm Industrial Estate,
Bagley Green, Wellington, Somerset TA21 9PZ
Tel: 01823 653777   Fax: 01823 216796
email: sales@halsgrove.com
website: www.halsgrove.com

Printed and bound by D'Auria Industrie Grafiche, Italy

CONTENTS

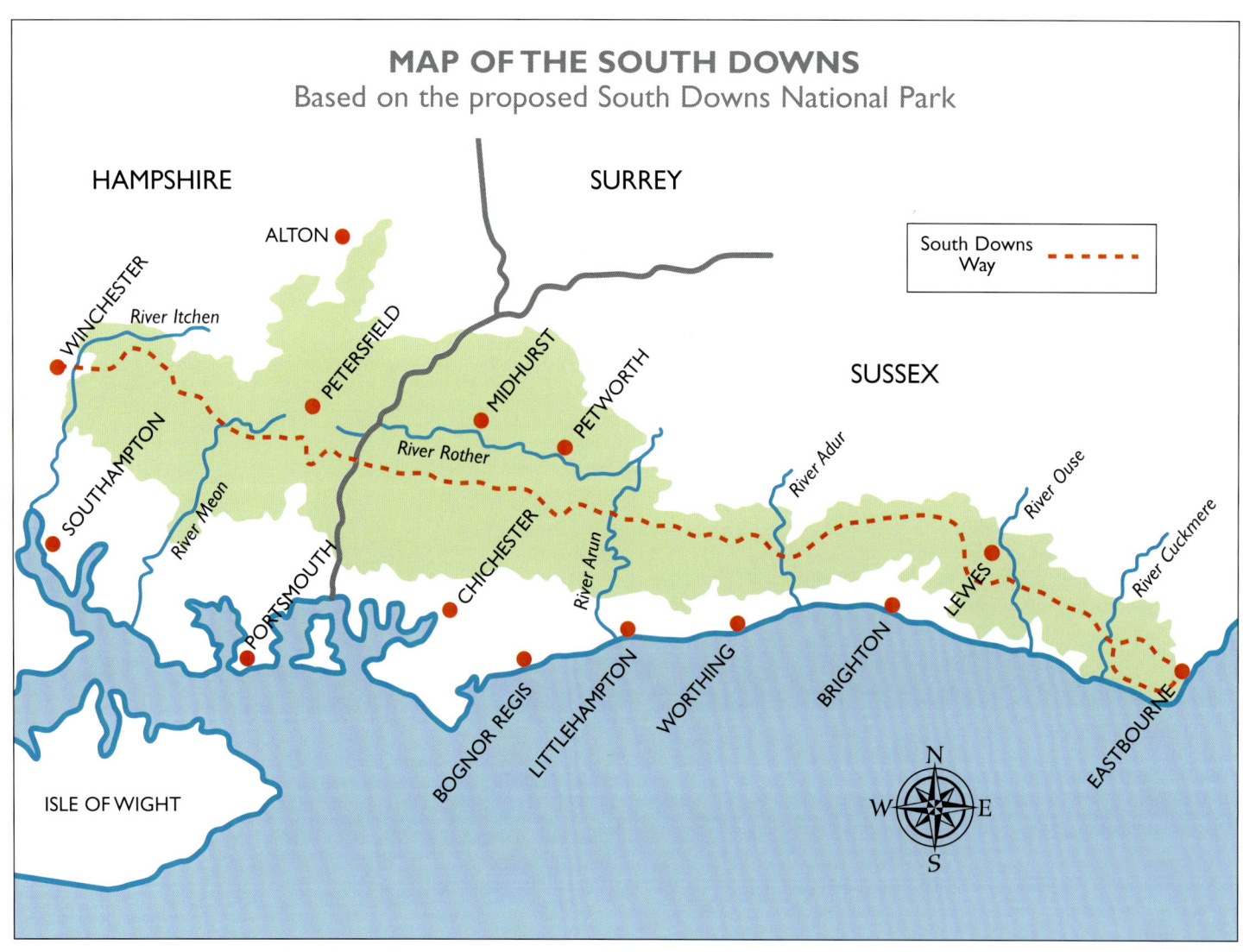

MAP OF THE SOUTH DOWNS
Based on the proposed South Downs National Park

HAMPSHIRE

SURREY

ALTON

WINCHESTER

River Itchen

SOUTHAMPTON

PETERSFIELD

MIDHURST

PETWORTH

SUSSEX

River Meon

River Rother

PORTSMOUTH

CHICHESTER

River Arun

River Adur

River Ouse

River Cuckmere

LEWES

BOGNOR REGIS

LITTLEHAMPTON

WORTHING

BRIGHTON

EASTBOURNE

ISLE OF WIGHT

South Downs Way	– – – –

N
W E
S

INTRODUCTION

We all have our own ideas and opinions on what constitutes and forms the classic, idyllic English landscape – a landscape that immediately springs to mind when we hear that one emotive word, England. For some it may be the storm-torn coastline and mysterious interior of Cornwall, for others the buttercup-stained field and walled patterns of the Yorkshire Dales. The vast empty expanses of Northumberland are often quoted, as are the calm, timeless, misty mornings of a Lake District dawn. And then of course there is the pastoral, visual heritage of Wessex – an ancient land of stone cottages set amongst steep hedge-lined hills or, perhaps, the flat fertile plains of East Anglia where the skies seem to stretch to infinity. But there is another landscape that has become familiar to most of us, made famous by numerous writers and artists throughout the centuries, a landscape often illustrated as evocative of England during the dark days of the Second World War. A landscape that stood for a certain indomitable spirit that we still pride ourselves on and one that can on occasions rouse our voices in emotional chorus – William Blake's 'England's Mountains green' – the South Downs. Of all the amazing variety of landscape forms within this tiny island, it is the South Downs that seem to hold a unique place in the English psyche, iconic, uplifting scenery, thought of as the quintessential England.

I have lived most of my life within sight of Kipling's 'blunt bow headed, whale backed Downs' and Belloc's 'great hills of the South Country'. They have formed a visual, spiritual and elemental backdrop to both work and pleasure and for many, a great escape. When I think of the Downs I think of the open vaulted skies, the song of the skylark, the gently rolling expanse of green or the classic chalk-land turf falling steeply on scarp slopes into mysterious half-hidden wooded coombes. I think of early mornings when the mist hangs low over the valleys or late evening light, with its long shadows, when the rounded outlines of the hills are bathed in a special texture. These hills with their elusive yet all pervading spirit, deep with a sense of history and place, have quite simply become some of the most famous and fondly regarded hills in the world.

But what of the future? At present most of the South Downs are included within the Sussex Downs and East Hampshire areas of Outstanding Natural Beauty and it is both of these that will be absorbed as the principal elements of the proposed South Downs National Park. This will be the first such park in South East England and will encompass not only the entire length of the Downs between the coastal resort of Eastbourne and Hampshire's historic city of Winchester but also an area in places extending from the very fringes of the generally built-up coastline to parts of the Surrey border in the north. This huge tract of land will include the entire main downland ridge together with much of the West Sussex and East Hampshire hinterland.

There is still considerable debate about these intentions but it is the extent of the proposed National Park that this book seeks to cover during a meandering photographic journey. A journey that takes in many of the dramatic views in their various moods plus the more intimate details of historic churches, villages, towns and archaeological sites to be found en route. This is a twenty-first century record of the living history of one of the nation's most admired landscapes, the South Downs.

Eastbourne seafront from the pier. As late as 1813 Eastbourne was noted as a small fashionable bathing place and it was not until the 1850s, on the initiative of the 7th Duke of Devonshire, that major development began following the earlier example of Brighton along the coast. With safe sands, a Victorian pier designed by Eugenius Birch and opened in 1872, a 5km, part three-tiered and flower-lined promenade backed by landscaped gardens, elegant hotels and large private houses, this distinguished town soon became affectionately known as 'Empress of the Watering Places'. The term is still used today and Eastbourne is now regarded as one of the finest resorts along the south coast. The pier itself is unusual in featuring a camera obscura, the technology of which dates back to the sixteenth century.

EASTBOURNE to THE OUSE VALLEY

The essential striped chairs of an English seaside resort

Any journey westwards along the South Downs begins at Eastbourne. Here on the very fringes of the town the rolling chalkland starts its great green sweep across Sussex and into Hampshire. For anyone walking the South Downs Way, the first long distance bridle-way to be designated by the Countryside Commission, the immediate prospect is an extremely stiff climb commencing quite literally at the end of Eastbourne's promenade. As with so many other landscape forms, the South Downs have their own distinctive sections and none more so than that from Eastbourne to the Ouse Valley where the bare, classic, open downland and softly rounded hills create a dramatic contrast to the more wooded countryside to be found later on during this journey. In addition it is here at this very early stage that the meeting of the Downs with the sea provides the unforgettable cliff scenery of Beachy Head and the Seven Sisters.

The Eastbourne seafront open-air bandstand concerts have become a highly popular attraction during the summer months. Various local and visiting brass and concert bands are all featured together with special events such as Rock 'n Roll nights, Proms nights, Tribute nights, firework concerts, Gilbert and Sullivan nights and big band nights. The bandstand itself, constructed in Art Deco style, was completed in 1935 and is noted for the excellent quality of its acoustics.

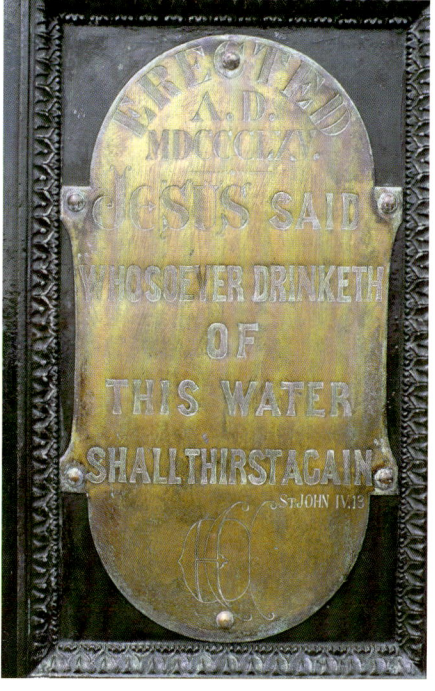

Seafront details.

Above: A brass plaque adorns a drinking fountain dated 1865.

Top left: Early nineteenth-century bow-fronted housing in what was once known as the hamlet of Seahouses.

Left: The Burlington Hotel dating from the 1850s.

Beachy Head. Immediately west of Eastbourne as the Downs meet the sea, the white chalk cliffs rise steeply to a height of 163m at Beachy Head. With the prominent red and white striped lighthouse below, the head has become one of the most famous landmarks in England. Away from the confines and habitation of Eastbourne, all is suddenly colour, light and space with wide ranging views out to sea and of the sheer precipitous cliff faces. After a long history of shipwrecks off the head, the eye catching lighthouse, completed in 1902, was the third to be built replacing the former Belle Tout lighthouse, now a private residence, and its predecessor dating back to 1828. Much of the labour and materials needed for the lighthouse were lowered via an aerial ropeway from the top of the cliffs.

On the sometimes almost inaccessible shoreline below the cliffs, beaches of bare chalk can be found together with considerable evidence of the constant erosion taking place as the ever-receding cliffs crumble at up to half a metre each year. Caves and ledges form a spectacular habitat for numerous sea birds.

The Seven Sisters from below Birling Gap. From Beachy Head westwards the perpendicular cliffs continue in a dazzling white undulating wall for almost 8km to Cuckmere Haven. Known as the Seven Sisters they form one of the most dramatic and celebrated sections of coastal scenery in Southern England. Along the top, the South Downs Way continues its journey to Winchester whilst at Birling Gap, with its stepped walkway to the beach, a hotel and a few houses brave the eroding cliff faces.

Late afternoon wintry light on one of the great iconic views of England and certainly of the South Downs and Sussex. Almost the entire length of the Seven Sisters cliffs can be seen here from Hope Gap below Seaford Head, ranging from Haven Brow in the west to Went Hill Brow in the east with the old Belle Tout lighthouse in the far distance. Beyond the foreground headland the River Cuckmere flows into the sea. The Cuckmere estuary, one of the few such undeveloped estuaries remaining along the south coast has now been incorporated within the Seven Sisters Country Park.

In less spectacular fashion our Downland journey from Eastbourne can also start by following the landward scarp slope of the Downs heading up on to the heights via Willingdon Hill, the village of Jevington and Windover Hill. An alternative South Downs Way route follows this course meeting up with the coastal section at Alfriston. The view shown here looks down from a shoulder of Windover Hill towards Folkington and the distant Pevensey Levels.

The rough flint and stone church of St Peter at Folkington was built about 1250 and despite its close proximity to the outskirts of Eastbourne has remained one of the most secluded churches in Sussex, lying with its small village at the foot of the Downs behind the parkland of Folkington Manor.

Light and shadows below Windover Hill. The nearby village of Wilmington contains the remains of a small Benedictine Priory suppressed in 1414 and now incorporated into a farmhouse. The Norman village church of St Mary and St Peter was at one time used both by the monks and the laity.

The Long Man of Wilmington. The 73m high Long Man with a staff in each hand cut out of the chalk downland of Windover Hill remains an enigma of uncertain age and purpose. He is possibly the largest outline of a human figure in Europe and undoubtedly the most well known of the chalk hill images in England. His history could go back 5000 years but his present stark appearance dates back only to the late nineteenth century being outlined within the chalk by white blocks. It is thought that originally he might have been holding a rake in one hand and a scythe in the other but this too is only conjecture.

Alfriston. The fourteenth-century timber-framed and thatched Clergy House at Alfriston was the first building to be purchased by the National Trust in 1896 for the grand sum of £10. It is a particularly fine example of a traditional Wealden 'Hall' house from this period. The house stands on the edge of the village green overlooking the River Cuckmere and next to the church of St Andrew known as the Cathedral of the Downs due to its size.

This brightly painted figurehead in the shape of a lion, rescued from a shipwreck some 300 years ago, stands outside the Star Inn at Alfriston. The half-timbered inn, one of the oldest in the country and dating back to about 1500, is famous for its association with smuggling. Alfriston itself with its many period buildings and stone market cross is a popular destination for visitors and walkers enjoying the village's downland location.

The Saxon village of Alciston lies at the end of a lane almost immediately below the northern slope of the Downs. At Court House Farm, incorporating Alciston Grange, is this magnificent 52m-long flint and tiled tithe barn, one of the longest in Sussex. The Grange was at one time the property of the wealthy Battle Abbey.

Adjacent to the barn are these remains of the medieval dovecot. Dovecots were once an important source of food during the long winters of the Middle Ages.

The twelfth-century church of St Michael and All Angels at Berwick almost certainly stands on a pre-Christian site but its main interest to visitors is the extraordinary set of paintings within by the artists Duncan Grant, Vanessa Bell and her children Quentin and Angelica. Due to wartime bombing a decorative scheme was commissioned to complement the installation of new plain glass windows rather than renewing the damaged leaded glass. The artists, who were living nearby at Charleston Farm, were chosen to carry out the work. Murals featuring the nativity and other scenes, which included local people and views, were painted on to plasterboard which was then fixed to the church walls, the scheme being dedicated in 1943. The photograph shows part of the nativity scene with Mount Caburn near Lewes in the background, local shepherds being asked to model, and complete with a Southdown lamb and Pyecombe crooks.

Charleston Farm, often known as Bloomsbury in Sussex, was the home of the artists Duncan Grant and Clive and Vanessa Bell from about 1916 onwards. Here an artistic, somewhat emotional, unconventional and bohemian partnership flourished where the seventeenth-century farmhouse fabric was literally transformed into a colourful canvas containing painted works, fabrics, pottery etc. Over the years the farm became a favourite retreat for others of the Bloomsbury Set and now forms an important part of twentieth-century artistic heritage. In recent years the house has been carefully restored by the Charleston Trust, together with the adjoining traditional English cottage garden, and is open to public viewing.

A glorious spring day on the Downs near Bostal Hill looking inland towards Charleston Farm and Kipling's 'wooded dim blue goodness of the Weald'. The word 'bostal' is an old Sussex name for a hill path.

Mist hangs over the Wealden fields below the 219m high Firle Beacon on an early summer's morning. This part of the Downs between Alfriston and Beddingham Hill has long been a favourite source of inspiration to writers and artists. Kipling wrote of 'our blunt, bow headed, whale backed Downs' with their 'bare slopes where chasing shadows skim' whilst the naturalist Gilbert White wrote in 1773 'Though I have now travelled the South Downs upwards of thirty years, yet I still investigate that chain of majestic mountains with fresh admiration year by year and think I see new beauties every time I traverse it!'.

A late winter's afternoon on the edge of the Downs.

The church of St Mary the Virgin in the village of Glynde was designed in Palladian style by Sir Thomas Robinson Bart for Richard Trevor, then Bishop of Durham and owner of the adjoining Glynde Place. It was completed in 1765, replacing an earlier church on the same site and is of a rare design for such a small parish church. The Georgian interior is of particular note containing original box pews, pulpit and reading desk and with the walls unusually covered in hessian. John Ellman, a gentleman farmer famous for breeding Southdown sheep, is buried in the churchyard. Glynde Place is an Elizabethan mansion originally built in 1569 for the Sussex ironmaster William Morley, whilst the world famous Glyndebourne Opera House, opened in 1934, is situated nearer the adjacent village of Ringmer.

Evening shadows spread across the fields at Firle viewed from near Firle Beacon. The prominent round tower on the left of the photograph was built in 1819 by the fourth Viscount Gage for his gamekeeper of the Firle Estate.

The Ouse Valley. For centuries the River Ouse was an important means of trade access from the coast to the Weald and on which much local prosperity depended. Southdown grain, wool and Wealden iron and timber would be sent down river to the port of Newhaven whilst more general groceries, textiles, spices etc were shipped northwards. Lewes, by the sixteenth and seventeenth centuries rapidly becoming the administrative centre of eastern Sussex, in particular benefited from its location by the river. During the early eighteenth century improvements were made to Newhaven harbour followed by substantial works on the river itself during the late eighteenth and early nineteenth centuries enabling navigable passage as far inland as Lindfield. The construction of this swing bridge over the widened and straightened river near Southease at one time provided the only crossing point for road traffic between Lewes and Newhaven.

The flint church of St Peter at Southease is one of only three Sussex churches built with a round tower, the others being St Michael at Lewes and St John at Piddinghoe further down the Ouse Valley. Having contracted in size over the years by the loss of its aisles and chancel, possibly due to the Black Death and a falling population, the church nevertheless celebrated 1000 years of recorded history in 1966. The small village of Southease is just one of several hamlets and villages situated along the lower Ouse Valley. Kingston, Iford, Northease, Rodmell, Piddinghoe, South Heighton, Tarring Neville, Itford and Beddingham all reflecting in their own way the once historic importance of this navigable waterway.

Monks House at Rodmell was once the country retreat of the novelist Virginia Woolf where she and her husband lived for more than twenty years until her death in 1941. Virginia's sister, the artist Vanessa Bell, lived in nearby Charleston Farm. The eighteenth-century Monks House, now owned by the National Trust, is of particular interest with its interiors that reflect the novelist's life and times. Rodmell was at one time spelt 'Rodmill' from the 'mill on the road' but no mill now exists in the village.

Storm clouds near Denton. Denton on the southern edge of the Downs almost opposite Newhaven was once a small downland hamlet with just a country church, manor house and a few flint cottages but together with neighbouring South Heighton has now become engulfed by suburban housing spreading out from Newhaven. It is however still an excellent starting point for the many different walks leading up on to the Downs where the wide-open vistas can be enjoyed at their best.

Lewes. The view looking down over the town's rooftops and St Michael's church from Lewes Castle towards the distant South Downs. Lewes, county town of East Sussex, is located mainly on a spur of the Downs above the River Ouse which flows through a narrowing gap in the hills on its way to the sea. Being a naturally strategic position, it was not long after the Norman Conquest before William de Warenne commenced a castle in about 1100 overlooking the river. Originally comprising two shell keeps on individual mounds, only the western keep has survived and still dominates the town as this view from its upper ramparts illustrates. As an ancient borough for many centuries, Lewes started to prosper from the late sixteenth century onwards becoming an important port and administration centre and later notable for its variety of architecture.

LEWES to AMBERLEY

Part of the remaining western keep of the castle as seen from the fourteenth-century barbican. The barbican, the last section of the castle to be built, is regarded as one of the finest of Its type In England.

The Downs between Lewes and Amberley pass north of some of the most densely populated areas of Sussex where almost the entire coastline has been developed. The towns of Newhaven, Peacehaven and City of Brighton & Hove, Shoreham, Worthing and Littlehampton form an almost continuous urban spread with much modern development encroaching upon the hills. Yet above all this the Downs can be as peaceful as ever, one can walk for hours without seeing another soul, just the ghosts of the past for company. For here surviving Iron Age hillforts, circular burial tumuli, downland trackways and many ancient churches still remind us of five thousand years of Sussex history.

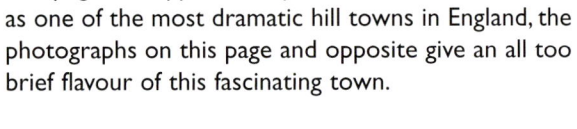

This page and opposite: Aspects of Lewes. Described as one of the most dramatic hill towns in England, the photographs on this page and opposite give an all too brief flavour of this fascinating town.

Bottom middle: The plaque commemorating the seventeen protestant martyrs burned at the stake here in the sixteenth century. *Below:* Part of the old quay area on the River Ouse at the bottom of the High Street. *Others:* Period buildings in the winding, descending High Street.

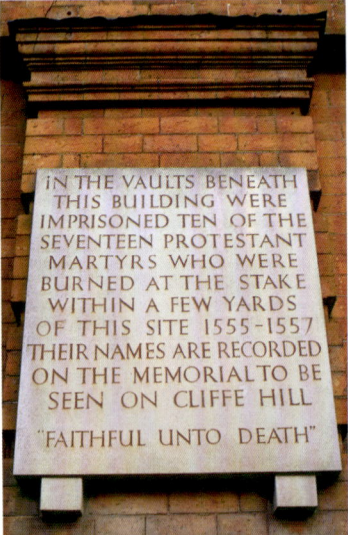

IN THE VAULTS BENEATH
THIS BUILDING WERE
IMPRISONED TEN OF THE
SEVENTEEN PROTESTANT
MARTYRS WHO WERE
BURNED AT THE STAKE
WITHIN A FEW YARDS
OF THIS SITE 1555-1557
THEIR NAMES ARE RECORDED
ON THE MEMORIAL TO BE
SEEN ON CLIFFE HILL

"FAITHFUL UNTO DEATH"

Left: The fourteenth-century barbican to the castle. In 1077 the Cluniac Priory of St Pancras was founded here but largely destroyed by Thomas Cromwell in 1538. It was thought to have been one of the most magnificent monasteries ever built in this country.

The lanes, 'twittens' and pedestrian alleys that drop sharply from the High Street to the lower town of Southover probably date from the planning of Lewes as a Saxon stronghold by King Alfred. *Above:* Cottages in the steeply graded Keere Street.

The outskirts of Brighton. Looking east from near Newmarket Hill back towards Lewes and illustrating the rural empty nature of the Downs even here on the very fringes of the City of Brighton & Hove.

The Chattri Indian War Memorial was erected near Patcham in 1921. Earlier on this site the bodies of Hindu and Sikh soldiers who had been wounded during the First World War and had then died in Brighton's Royal Pavilion, at that time an emergency hospital, were cremated their ashes being scattered over the sea. Designed by the Hindu architect E. C. Henriques, constructed from Sicilian marble and unveiled by HRH Prince of Wales, the memorial was renovated thirty years later by the Patcham Branch of the Royal British Legion. An annual pilgrimage and memorial service organised by the Legion has been held every year since, attended by the High Commissioner for India or his representative, Indian officers and members of the Legion.

The well-known windmills of Jack and Jill high on the Downs above Clayton are one of the county's best loved features and a notable sight to downland walkers and passengers travelling by train to Brighton. The white painted Jill, a timber post mill, was originally built about 1820 and sited nearer Brighton but later dismantled and moved to its present position in the mid-nineteenth century having been hauled across the Downs by teams of oxen. Jack, in the background, is a brick built tower mill constructed in the late 1890s and now a private residence. Jill, in the care of the Jack and Jill Windmill Society is open to the public on a limited basis.

Looking north from the slopes of Ditchling Beacon, inland across the Weald. At 248m, the beacon is the highest point in East Sussex and was one of the sites where fires were lit to warn of the Armada four centuries ago. The earthwork remains of an Iron Age hillfort surround the beacon with magnificent views all around. The village of Ditchling below has become famous for the artists and craftsmen who have lived there including the well-known sculptor, typographer and writer Eric Gill.

The Devil's Dyke. The Dyke, Dyke Hill and adjacent Downs have been a popular beauty spot for many years and in particular for visitors from Brighton nearby. The Dyke itself, a steep curving valley, is said to have been formed by the Devil in his attempt to dig a trench through the Downs and so flood the Wealden churches but was thwarted without completing the task. Dyke Hill offers glorious views to the counties of Hampshire, Kent and Surrey on a clear day and is now extremely popular for hang gliding and parascending. At one time a railway branch line terminated near here from Brighton, an aerial cableway spanned the valley and a funicular railway on the north slope of Dyke Hill descended to Poynings.

Pyecombe's village sign illustrates traditional Southdown sheep in a downland setting complete with a Pyecombe crook. The distinctively designed crooks were made at Pyecombe Forge and carried all over the nearby chalk hills by the old shepherds of the Downs in the early years of the nineteenth century. During this period it is estimated that up to a quarter of a million ewes could be found grazing between Eastbourne and Steyning, a form of land management that has long since disappeared in favour of planted crops.

The donkey wheel at Saddlescombe Farm inside its weather boarded house is now in the care of Brighton & Hove City Council. It is one of only a very few such wheels remaining and would have been worked by a single donkey or even two men to raise wooden buckets from the 53m well. It probably dates back to the eighteenth century and was known to still be in use around 1910.

Water still gushes vigorously out of the chalk at this roadside spring below the Downs at Fulking. At one time the village was synonymous with the down-land sheep flocks and the spring used for washing the sheep prior to the annual shearing, its clear water being ideal for the purpose. The adjacent Shepherd & Dog Inn would once have been filled with shepherds, their dogs and the shearing gangs relaxing after many a hard day spent here.

Towards the River Adur. The chapel of Lancing College was designed by R. C. Carpenter in an early English Gothic style with French influences and construction commenced in 1868. It was built to serve the Woodard School of Lancing College and act as a central Minster for the entire Woodard Federation. As one of the tallest churches in England and designated as a national monument, the spectacular soaring chapel as seen today was finally completed in 1911 long after the death of the original architect and Nathaniel Woodard himself. An intended north tower and west end have never been built. The Sussex sandstone chapel with its 30m high interior is situated on a sloping, exposed site on the edge of the Downs next to the school and overlooking the Adur Valley. It required foundations of some 20m in depth. Nathaniel Woodard's aim was to found a comprehensive and classless, less exclusive, federation of schools independent of the state system. There are now over thirty of these schools of which Lancing, Ardingly and Hurstpierpoint are all in Sussex.

The interior of the undedicated church at Coombes on the western flank of the Adur Valley features some of the finest Norman paintings to be found in Sussex. They were discovered in 1949 and are thought to date back to around 1130. The church itself, tucked into the hills, was probably constructed in the late eleventh century but fortunately untouched during the Victorian era. As such Pevsner describes the building as 'lovable and unrestored - a century by century accretion of piety'.

Doorway carving, the church of St Botolph at Botolphs. The tiny depopulated hamlet of Botolphs lies just a mile north of Coombes within the Adur Valley. Around a thousand years ago a bridge spanned the river near the church with an adjacent flourishing community serving the Manor of Annington. As the then wide river silted up over the centuries and the sea receded, the village lost its prosperity and much of its population and today there are fewer than fifty residents. The church with much Saxon construction dates back to around 950, a north aisle being added during the thirteenth century only to be subsequently demolished later as the village declined. The church is now incorporated within the parish of 'Beeding and Bramber with Botolphs' and the photograph shows a detail of the oak door with the date 1630 carved on it.

Norman arches, St Andrew's church, Steyning. This outstanding Norman church is built on the site of an earlier Saxon timber structure and reflects Steyning's then importance as a port on the Adur. The building has been referred to as 'the most majestic fragment of twelfth-century ecclesiastical architecture in Sussex' and 'among the best in the entire country'. Although much was demolished after the reformation, the Romanesque nave was left intact with its magnificently carved arches to both north and south aisles and chancel and massive supporting cylindrical piers. It is known that King Ethelwulf, the father of King Alfred, was buried in the original Saxon church and it is thought that one of the surviving Saxon coffin lids on display in the present building could have perhaps covered his grave.

A late winter's afternoon at Chanctonbury Ring. This Iron Age hillfort planted with beech trees in 1760 by Charles Goring, became one of the best known and most distinctive profiles of the South Downs. Decimated by the great storm of 1987, the ring has now been replanted and it is hoped that one day it will again be looked upon as one of the great sights of Sussex. From its summit almost all of Sussex can be seen with parts of Hampshire, Kent and Surrey in addition. As the centre of numerous local legends, particularly on moonless nights, the ring is thought to have been a sacred place in Neolithic times. Local people still tell of curious sensations when up at the Ring and of unexplainable actions of horses and dogs when in its vicinity.

The fringes of Worthing. Winter on Cissbury Ring. Cissbury Ring is one of the largest Iron Age hillforts in Southern England enclosing an area of some 26 hectares. Situated about 4km to the south of Chanctonbury Ring and on the very edge of Findon near Worthing, it contains within its earthen banks the remains of some 200 Neolithic flint mines thought to have been worked over 4000 years ago. The mines consisting of vertical shafts with radiating galleries would have been dug with antler picks, shovels of oxen shoulder blades and other flint tools, all of which have been discovered on the site and are now housed in Worthing Museum. As such the area forms one of the earliest industrial complexes in Britain. Similar mining evidence can also be found on nearby Blackpatch and Harrow Hills.

Downs, sheep and sky. A view looking eastwards from near Cissbury Ring back towards Steyning and illustrating the nature of the wide open downland in this vicinity.

The Great Sussex Sheep Fair at Findon is thought to have been held during most Septembers since the thirteenth century when a charter was granted by Henry III in 1261. Up to 20,000 sheep are often taken to the fair from all over Sussex and at one time cattle, donkeys, horses and goats would also have been sold. Stories are still told of the days when the sheep would have been driven to the fair along the old drove roads, many of which survive as downland tracks. The date of the fair was also considered to be the day when winter fires would be lit. As well as a serious business for farmers, the fair has traditionally been regarded as a great day out with its side shows, amusements, fortune telling and boxing booths. Fair nights at the local inns and pubs were said to be occasions to be remembered.

St Mary's church at Sompting is totally unique. On the edge of Worthing where the Downs meet the coastal plain, it is the only church in the country to feature a gabled pyramidal cap, or four-gabled spire, to its Saxon tower. Often termed a 'Rhenish Helm' it is named after similar structures to be found in Germany and along the Rhine. The tower itself with its characteristic pilaster strips is dated to about 1000 whilst most of the remainder of the church was rebuilt in the late twelfth century by the Knights Templar. Passing to the Knights Hospitallers, or Knights of St John in the early fourteenth century, the church was extended by a further chapel, now in ruins. The order of St John was later revived as the St John's Ambulance Association which now has many connections with the church.

The beautiful Elizabethan mansion of Parham House stands in its Tudor landscaped deer park overlooking the Downs just west of Storrington. With magnificent views, the house was built in 1577 and is particularly well known for its Great Hall featuring windows some 7m high and its top floor Long Gallery almost 49m long. The house contains a superb collection of paintings and furniture and what has been described as the finest collection of needlework in any house in England. St Peter's church, dating back to 1545, stands in the park near the house complete with intact box pews, a separate squire's pew with fireplace and a unique fourteenth-century lead font. The house was opened to the public in 1948 and now, owned by a Charitable Trust and with its award winning gardens, is a highly popular location for visitors.

This page and opposite: Amberley. The exceptionally attractive village of Amberley stands at the foot of the Downs escarpment and features numerous stone, flint and traditional half-timbered cottages many of which are thatched and surrounded by old-fashioned cottage gardens. With its Norman church and fourteenth-century castle, the village is often considered to be one of the prettiest in Sussex and popular with artists.

The variations in cottage styles and materials give a certain romantic appeal to the village and always more so during the summer months when on certain weekends the cottage gardens are open to visitors. The partly-ruined castle is now run as a top-class country hotel.

Southdown Bus Garage, Amberley Working Museum. The museum is set in a disused chalk quarry that was at one time served by the adjacent Amberley railway station. The open-air museum contains exhibits illustrating and describing many facets of the industrial history of South East England including the process of lime production for which the chalk quarry was used for over 100 years until its closure in the 1960s. An industrial narrow gauge railway or vintage bus take visitors around the 15 hectare site which features a large collection of road transport, telecommunications exhibition, electricity hall, printing works, bus garage, lime kilns, traditional crafts and numerous other exhibits and attractions. Throughout the year many temporary exhibitions, special days and outdoor events are also held such as vintage car, cycle and motorcycle shows, a railway gala weekend, craft days, home front celebrations, rallies, science workshops, classic car picnics and much more. As one of the South's leading attractions, there is something here to suit everyone.

To the north and east of Amberley village lie the Amberley Wild Brooks, a series of water meadows of dyke-drained pasture and scrub that at one time provided grazing and hay for farmers' livestock over the centuries. In winter the Brooks are often completely flooded by the winding River Arun but in summer they are a haven for insects, birds, flowers and wetland plant species. The photograph shows the flooded Brooks on a grey, still winter's morning.

North Stoke church interior. North Stoke church in a rural setting on the lower slopes of the Downs within a loop of the River Arun remains unaltered since medieval times, the identity of its patron saint having long been lost, and is now in the care of the Churches Conservation Trust. In the simple shape of a cross and with a Norman nave, thirteenth-century transepts, fourteenth-century chancel and some outstanding window designs, the church's elegant proportions give an impression of light and space within. Pevsner described the interior as 'a wonderful atmospheric blend of white, yellow and faded red, lit by clear glass'. Traces of fourteenth-century paintings illustrate flowers, leaves and scrolls whilst tiny fragments of very rare early stained glass, also from the fourteenth century, are present in some of the windows. As described in the Trust's informative leaflet, the church is a 'memorable combination of rustic charm, fine architecture and an atmosphere of prayer'.

The River Arun seen from the new bridge carrying the South Downs Way across the river near Houghton. Once a busy waterway, the river was the only one in Sussex suitable for barges to navigate any significant distance into the Weald up to the early years of the eighteenth century. By the end of the same century further improvements had been carried out culminating in the opening of the Wey & Arun Junction Canal in 1816 and the Arundel & Portsmouth Canal in 1823. The combination of canal and river enabled a continuous line of navigation to be used between London and Portsmouth and later to be known as 'London's lost route to the sea'. As with so many similar schemes, after modestly trading for some fifty years, the coming of the railways heralded the decline of the river's fortunes and with closure of both canals during the latter half of the nineteenth century, the river almost entirely ceased to act as a commercial waterway. Today it is only used for private boating and pleasure cruises from Arundel and Littlehampton. The river is also noted for its extremely strong currents with a tidal flow on its lower reaches, which is one of the fastest in England.

Arundel Castle. The ancient town of Arundel, situated on a ridge sloping down to the River Arun and where the Downs meet the coastal plain, has one of the most dramatic skylines in England. Seen from the south Arundel is dominated by its castle, cathedral and parish church with period, closely-knit housing, stepping down to the water's edge. The castle, ancestral home of the Dukes of Norfolk mainly dates from an almost total rebuilding between 1890 and 1903. Fragments of the original castle, ruined during the Civil War and dating back to 1067 remain, including the keep and barbican from the twelfth and thirteenth centuries respectively. Rebuilt in a Gothic style and on a grandiose scale not dissimilar to Windsor Castle, it is impressive simply by size and location.

ARUNDEL to HARTING

A detail of Hiorn's Tower built in 1790 within Arundel Park to a triangular plan and noted for its chequer-patterned elevations of flint and stone. The park of some 500 hectares extends north from the castle up and on to the Downs with glorious views particularly across the Arun Valley.

From Arundel to Harting the nature of the South Downs begins to change from the relatively bare and open, softly-rounded hills in the east to a more wooded and broader upland. Here the trees often mask the very profiles of the slopes and valleys whilst along the northern escarpment with its defined ridge, hanging woods create a unique environment rich in wildlife. To the south evidence of coppicing, deer parks, coverts and rabbit warrens illustrate a way of life, partly from a sporting and estate tradition, that is at present in a considerable degree of flux. This is the country beloved of the great Sussex writer Hillaire Belloc who once wrote:

When I am living in the Midlands
That are sodden and unkind ....
The great hills of the South Country
Come back into my mind.

A freshly sown mantle of winter wheat clothes the lower slopes of Bury Hill. The South Downs Way passes near here on its long ascent from the Arun Valley up to the summit of Bignor Hill.

A misty early October morning view from Bury Hill looking down towards the Arun Valley. The writer John Galsworthy lived nearby at Bury House and after his death his ashes were scattered on the hill. The mist hanging in the valley is a common sight during the autumn and winter months.

Evocative downland textures on Bury and Bignor Hills. Much of the old chalk grassland, synonymous with the grazing of Southdown sheep has disappeared over the years in favour of high-yield cereal crops with all the risks of soil erosion and flooding that this policy entails. There are, however, limited new moves away from this trend with the introduction of grants to farmers to encourage reinstatement of grassland with its allied benefits to wildlife, bio-diversity and the environment generally. It is the hope of many that this initiative will continue.

A sense of infinity, a study of yellow, white and blue with fields of oilseed rape under late spring skies. The crop is just one of several more colourful crops to be found on the Downs and often referred to as England's Yellow Peril since it is such a distinctive feature of the rural landscape at this time of year.

Walkers head east over Bignor Hill during the twenty-seventh annual South Downs Way Walk in 2006 organised by Footprints of Sussex on behalf of West Sussex County Council. The walk takes place over nine consecutive days covering the entire distance from Eastbourne to Winchester with up to 200 people taking part. The Arun Valley with Amberley Mount and the Amberley Wild Brooks wetlands and much of the West Sussex Downs can be seen in the distance. The designation of the South Downs Way was a milestone in walking history and with its later extension to Winchester the route is now 160km long and has become one of the most popular of all long distance walks in this country. Numerous clubs, societies and groups organise walks over its whole distance and individual walkers can be seen virtually every day of the year in any weather conditions along its length.

Downland activities. Apart from walking, the Downs are particularly popular for horse riding and off-road cycling, with a limited few also undertaking Llama trekking. Artists, composers, photographers and writers have all sought inspiration over the centuries from these hills, many producing works that we now regard as a part of our national being and heritage. These three illustrations are taken on Bignor Hill.

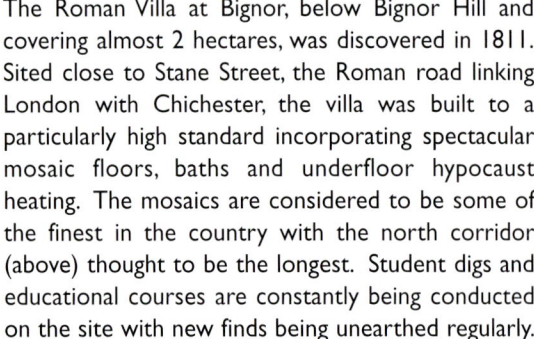

The Roman Villa at Bignor, below Bignor Hill and covering almost 2 hectares, was discovered in 1811. Sited close to Stane Street, the Roman road linking London with Chichester, the villa was built to a particularly high standard incorporating spectacular mosaic floors, baths and underfloor hypocaust heating. The mosaics are considered to be some of the finest in the country with the north corridor (above) thought to be the longest. Student digs and educational courses are constantly being conducted on the site with new finds being unearthed regularly.

Winter snow on Bignor Hill. Approaching from the west, Bignor Hill offers one of the first great classic views from its summit of the rolling Downs ahead as they stretch towards East Sussex and the distant but often prominent Woolstanbury Hill and Ditchling Beacon.

A late winter's afternoon in Eartham Woods. The Roman Stane Street passes though the woods on its route to Chichester whilst at nearby Slindon the writer Hillaire Belloc lived for many years. The National Trust's Slindon Estate comprises some 1500 hectares of wood and farmland extending to the northern escarpment of the Downs and including Bignor Hill and Glatting Beacon.

The prominent landmark of Halnaker Mill was built in the late eighteenth century replacing an earlier structure first recorded in 1540. After falling into disrepair, the mill was restored externally in 1934 as a memorial to the wife of Sir William Bird who lived nearby, although the interior remains an empty shell. The windmill has been immortalised in a passionate poem *Ha'nacker Mill* by Hillaire Belloc and later put to music by Christopher Le Fleming, where its once ruined condition was compared to the decay of English agriculture.

Sally is gone that was so kindly
Sally is gone from Ha'nacker Hill
And the Briar grows ever since then so blindly
And ever since then the clapper is still

Ha'nacker Hill is in Desolation
Ruin a'top and a field unploughed
And spirits that call on a fallen nation
Spirits that loved her calling aloud.

The church of St Mary the Virgin, Upwaltham in wintry fields. Described by Pevsner as 'untouched and lovable', the church dates back to the twelfth century with only later window and detailing alterations. It is particularly noted for its apsidal chancel and east end, of which only three others remain in Sussex. Cardinal Manning, who was once curate to the rector of nearby Graffham, wrote 'the Hills ….. Upwaltham Church ….. the Downs seem to me only less beautiful than Heaven'. In over 1000 years, the church will have seen little change in this rural area.

A view from near Barlavington Down looking north to Petworth and Northchapel. Blackdown can be seen in the far distance.

Summer skies, fields and poppies near St Roche's Hill. The hill, with its Iron Age hillfort known as The Trundle, commands spectacular views in all directions including the Goodwood Race Course and the more distant city of Chichester on the coastal plain.

A winter downland landscape below Charlton Down near the Goodwood Race Course.

Crowds enjoy the summer sunshine on top of The Trundle overlooking the Goodwood Race Course. Racing at Goodwood was begun by the 3rd Duke of Richmond in 1801 and with the later erection of a grandstand and subsequent eighteenth century improvements, the meetings soon became an important event in the social calendar. It was King Edward VII's sentiment that racing at Goodwood 'is a garden party with racing tacked on' that has been endorsed over the years by race goers and which has created the unique Goodwood atmosphere still to be found today. With magnificent views over the Downs, the course is being updated constantly with new stands and facilities and with the introduction of evening and Sunday racing is as popular as ever. 'Glorious Goodwood' week during July is still regarded by many as the place to be and to be seen and is a notable feature of the English summer season.

The Cass Sculpture Foundation at Goodwood is a charity recognised internationally as the home of twenty-first century British sculpture. Founded and privately endowed by Wilfred and Jeannette Cass in 1994, the charity's objective is to enhance the public enjoyment and appreciation of the strength and quality of British sculpture. To date more than 140 large-scale sculptures have been commissioned from over 120 artists and every year about one third of the work moves on to new homes around the world making space for further commissions. Situated in an idyllic venue of woodland walks and glades, the photographs show a few aspects of the remarkable sculpture to be found here.

This page and opposite: The Weald and Downland Open Air Museum at Singleton was established in the late 1960s and is now the leading museum of historic buildings in England. Set in 20 hectares of pasture and woodland on the edge of the Downs, the museum's aim is to encourage public interest in the rich heritage of vernacular buildings in South East England. The museum is constantly developing and its 45 rescued and recreated buildings represent the traditional homes and work-places of village and countryside over six centuries. An ambitious programme in building conservation and rural skills is offered to professionals and interested individuals together with educational courses for schools. In interpreting the build-ings, these are supported by period gardens, farm livestock, exhibitions, skills' demonstrations and numerous special events with countryside themes. The small staff and teams of enthusiastic volunteers provide a rewarding experience of recreation and education to the thousands of visitors who come here each year.

One of the thousands of ancient yew trees to be found in Kingley Vale National Nature Reserve. The vale, northwest of Chichester, is famous for its great yew forest often described as the finest in Europe. At the turn of the nineteenth century the writer E. V. Lucas wrote 'Kingley Vale always grave and silent is transformed at dusk into a sinister and fantastic forest, the home for witchcraft and unquiet spirits'. Apart from the forest the reserve contains a wide range of archaeological remains including a group of Bronze Age tumuli known as the Devil's Jumps on top of Bow Hill.

The view from The Trundle on St Roche's Hill looking down on to the City of Chichester and its prominent cathedral. In the far distance the coastal plain extends, as the Manhood Peninsula, to the sea. It is thought that the Iron Age hillfort surmounting the hill was abandoned in about 100BC. Later during the Middle Ages a chapel dedicated to St Roche was built on the hilltop followed by a windmill destroyed by fire in the late eighteenth century. On a clear day much of West Sussex, parts of Hampshire and the Isle of Wight can be seen from this outstanding viewpoint.

Racton Monument. The ghostly remains of this monument, not far from Kingley Vale, and known locally as Racton Tower, were once a folly built for Lord Halifax, owner of Stansted Park, in 1772. Designed by Theodosius Keene, the folly was a pleasure house and later a haunt of smugglers who could signal from the top of the tower to waiting boats loaded with contraband in Chichester harbour.

The interior of the thirteenth-century church of St Michael, Up Marden. Situated in a remote hamlet high up on the Downs, this church has been described by Pevsner as having 'one of the loveliest interiors in England. A visible loving testimony of the faith of successive generations'. Simon Jenkins, in his book *England's Thousand Best Churches* refers to the 'brick floor, box pews and wooden benches' as a 'study in tranquillity'. In Jenkin's words 'the churches of the Sussex Downs merit a book to themselves. They are the simplest religious structures in England, begun by pious Saxons and Normans and mostly left alone in their poverty even by the Victorians'.

Looking east along the Downs escarpment from Beacon Hill towards Treyford and Didling Hills and Cocking Down. The minute church of St Andrew at Didling, situated immediately below the scarp slope, is known as the Shepherd's Church and is another fine example of a totally unspoilt thirteenth-century building in Sussex.

Uppark House is one of the finest country houses within the South Downs. Enjoying dramatic views to the Isle of Wight from high on the hills near South Harting, the house was built about 1690, later being remodelled by the Fetherstonhaugh family at various periods. It was furnished in grand fashion reflecting the family's travels around the world and in this condition remained unaltered from the mid-nineteenth century until the disastrous fire in 1989 that totally gutted the interior. After the fire the National Trust, who by then owned the property, took the brave decision to restore the house to its pre-fire condition, this being finally achieved when Uppark was re-opened to visitors in 1995 after a remarkable restoration programme.

Village festivities at South Harting. Fêtes and festivities of all descriptions together with horticultural shows and fund-raising events for churches, village halls, schools and other needy projects take place each weekend through-out the summer months in most downland villages. Sometimes several events occur on the same day particularly in the month of June and for any ardent fête enthusiast, difficult decisions have to be made! What is common however is the great enthusiasm and community spirit to be found during all these occasions.

A popular view from Harting Down looking towards the village of South Harting and its copper-clad church spire with the Hampshire border beyond. This area of downland is owned by the National Trust and is a designated Site of Special Scientific Interest. W. H. Hudson considered the village to be the most attractive of all downland villages and it is particularly notable for many of its older buildings being constructed in the distinctive local chalky-white clunch stone. Note also the old winding track or Bostal leading up on to the Downs from below.

Blackdown at 280m is the highest point in Sussex. As a lofty sandstone ridge it overlooks most of the West Sussex Weald and Downs together with parts of neighbouring Surrey and Hampshire. Many of the views, particularly across the Weald as shown here, illustrate the degree of woodland still surviving in this area. At nearby Aldsworth House Tennyson wrote his famous lines:

You came, and looked and loved the view
Long known and loved by me,
Green Sussex fading into blue
With one grey glimpse of sea.

BLACKDOWN, PETWORTH and MIDHURST

Stopham Bridge spanning the River Arun near its junction with the Western River Rother, close to Pulborough, originates from 1309 and was later rebuilt in 1423. Regarded as one of the finest medieval bridges in Sussex, the centre arch was raised in 1822 to accommodate barges using the Wey & Arun Canal and the Rother Navigation.

Between the Arun Valley and the Hampshire border, the area encompassed by the Sussex Downs Area of Outstanding Natural Beauty, and likely to be incorporated within the proposed South Downs National Park, broadens northwards away from the main Downs escarpment. Stretching as far as Blackdown and the Surrey borders, the scenery changes totally, being based on a sandstone formation rather than chalk. This contrasting, remarkably diverse 'secret' countryside with its many commons, heaths, woodlands and distant views back to the Downs has its own distinctive hilly character where the grey/buff stone has become a prominent building material. The two principal towns of Petworth and Midhurst are both linked by the Western River Rother, at one time navigable as far as Midhurst Quay.

Looking across Petworth rooftops towards Petworth House. The town of Petworth has developed in the shadow of the great house and park and described by Cobbett in 1823 as 'a nice market town, but solid and clean'. Despite invasive traffic it is still a pleasure to walk around, revealing an abundance of local vernacular styles and materials with often delightful small gardens or courtyards just visible behind walls and gates. St Mary's parish church, seen on the right of the photograph once had a spire which was taken down in 1947 and which had led to the verse 'Proud Petworth, Poor people, High Church, Crooked Steeple'. In recent times the town has established itself as one of Southern England's leading centres for antiques and together with its house, park and museums has become a popular destination for visitors.

The striking west front of Petworth House in its parkland setting was built during the latter years of the seventeenth century as part of the great remodelling of the house by the 6th Duke of Somerset, who engaged master craftsmen such as the wood carver Grinling Gibbons to work on the building's magnificent interior. The house incorporates the chapel, constructed in 1309, of the original fortified house that stood on the site. One of the glories of the house is its magnificent collection of paintings including works by Gainsborough, Rembrandt, Turner and Vandyke. During the 1750s Lancelot 'Capability' Brown landscaped the deer park on a grand scale, considered to be one of his finest creations and the inspiration for some of Turner's paintings. The house and park were given to the National Trust shortly after the Second World War but the 2nd Lord Egremont, descendant of the Egremont line, his family still live in their ancestral home.

Heavy horses and a binder at work at the Northchapel Steam Fair. Northchapel was at one time a major centre for the Sussex glass and iron industries, charcoal manufacture and apple growing, but is now a rural village on the Petworth to Chiddingfold road. A tollhouse was built here shortly after road improvements to Petworth but closed in 1871 following the abolition of most road tolls. The village's name is derived from a church or chapel being built north of Petworth.

In West Lavington churchyard lies the body of Richard Cobden. Born in 1804, Cobden became a successful businessman and travelled extensively before entering Parliament in 1841. In a decade often referred to as the 'Hungry Forties', he became leader of the Anti-Corn Law League and a national hero when the Corn Laws were repealed in 1845. He died in 1865 and this tablet was erected by his family above his pew in St James' church, Heyshott. His former home at Dunford, close to neighbouring Midhurst, is now used as a conference centre and belongs to the YMCA.

SCROPE

FITZALAN·COMES   ARUNDELI

Within the eleventh-century church of St James at Selham is a set of magnificently-coloured stained glass windows installed by the Rev. Robert Blackburn, Victorian rector of Selham for 57 years. He was immensely proud that his wife could trace her ancestry back to the Plantagenets and the thought of the historic bloodline being carried on by his children. As a result the windows were designed to incorporate illustrations of his children's ancestral heraldic shields as shown here. The windows are remarkable for their dense colouration and have been described as having a jewel-like quality especially when sunlight passes through.

On the north bank of the River Rother lie the battlemented ruins of Cowdray House gutted by fire in 1793. Built about 1520, the building was reached by a raised causeway from nearby Midhurst and was once a magnificent Tudor mansion, its ivy clad remains being preserved in their 250-hectare parkland setting together with the almost intact kitchen that survived the fire. Synonymous with Cowdray Park and Midhurst, the game of polo was first played here in 1910. Considered to be one of the oldest recorded games in the world, it has become a frequent pastime of royalty, many members of which have played at Cowdray over the years.

Midhurst grew through the centuries on the south bank of the River Rother to become an important market town and it is possible to trace its development through its attractive and traditional buildings ranging from fifteenth-century timber framing to elegant Georgian brick or local stone. There was once a castle here built by the Normans but which was abandoned in the thirteenth century and around which the town's plan was originally based. Prominent in South Street is the Spread Eagle Hotel, on the left of the photograph, claiming to date back to 1430 but added to around 1700 and once well known as a coaching inn. Opposite the hotel is the old sixteenth-century Tudor Market Hall that served initially as a covered market place and later as a schoolroom for the newly-founded Grammar School. This continued until the re-founding of the school on a different site in 1881. Pupils of the school included the novelist H. G. Wells, later to teach there, the politician and economist Richard Cobden and the geologist Charles Lyell.

The road bridge over the Rother at Stedham is thought to be of seventeenth-century origin and is just one of several historic bridges on the upper reaches of the river. A cast iron plate dated 1912 and still in position issues a stern warning from the West Sussex County Council that locomotives are not allowed to stand on any part of the bridge.

Early spring in Hammer Wood near Chithurst. The wood is typical of so many others within this region, often in secluded valleys and comprising a quite dense variety of tree species with a woodland floor carpeted with bluebell and other spring flowers.

The eleventh-century church of St Mary at Chithurst stands on a knoll, possibly a pre-Christian site, above the banks of the Rother. This tiny and simplest of churches has changed little over an entire millennium and Pevsner quotes 'that poverty or remoteness have kept the original dimensions intact without any kind of addition'. Some of the surrounding grave slabs are claimed to be nearly as old as the church itself.

The church of St George at Trotton is famous for its wall paintings and medieval brasses. On the west wall are featured paintings of the last judgement and the photograph here shows the 'region of the blessed' with a clothed man and seven works of mercy. The paintings have been dated to around 1380 and would at one time have decorated the entire building. The church's magnificent brasses include that of Margaret Camoys, the earliest known brass of a woman, from about 1310 and the table tomb illustration of Thomas, Lord Camoys, a hero of Agincourt, and his wife Elizabeth dated around 1419. Noted as one of the largest, most ornate and best preserved brasses in England, an image of the latter brass has been embroidered on one of the colourful collection of kneelers.

Shulbrede Priory near Linchmere close to the northern boundary of the district with Surrey, was founded at around the turn of the thirteenth century for five canons of the Augustinian order. After the Dissolution it became a farm and at the beginning of the twentieth century was converted and lovingly restored into a private home by the MP Arthur Ponsonby and his wife Dorothea, daughter of the composer Hubert Parry. One of the building's best known features is the series of sixteenth-century wall paintings showing ladies in Elizabethan costumes and animals celebrating the Nativity.

This page and opposite: Colour at Hollycombe. The Hollycombe Steam Collection, just within the Sussex border near Liphook, is Britain's largest collection of working steam. Steam-driven fairground rides and attractions, steam narrow gauge industrial railways, steam-powered road rollers and traction engines, steam farm equipment and machinery are all featured together with woodland gardens, farm animals and an education and visitor centre.

The collection is owned by a charitable trust and open to visitors during limited periods of the year. Special events are often held including commercial vehicle gatherings, magic lantern shows, children's days, railway weekends, fairground nights and festivals of steam. The photographs here give a brief flavour of the colour and interest to be found at this fascinating venue.

Milland old church. Known as the Tuxlith Chapel, the building is thought to date from the eleventh century but completely refurbished in the fifteenth century and enlarged and much altered in the 1830s. It ceased to be used regularly after consecration of the adjacent new church of St Luke in 1879 and by the 1940s the chapel was a dangerous ruin with part of the roof having collapsed. In 1972 the building was declared redundant and taken over by the Friends of Friendless Churches who, working with the Friends of Tuxlith Chapel, have carried out much needed maintenance and restoration work. This simple and humble building, resembling more a Welsh chapel than a Sussex church, with its box pews and plain pulpit is a rarity in Southern England. Despite its close proximity to the old A3 Portsmouth road, the chapel still has a feeling of complete remoteness amongst the surrounding trees.

The view from the 183m high Older Hill looking over Redford and Woolbeding Common to the distant South Downs. Consisting of open woodland, Woolbeding Common is similar to many of the other commons to be found in this hilly region to the north and west of Midhurst. This together with Iping, Midhurst, Pound and Stedham commons is typical of Sussex Greensand heathland.

Into Hampshire. The isolated St Hubert's chapel at Idsworth stands alone in fields not far from the Sussex border and close to the Queen Elizabeth Country Park. Built in the mid eleventh century, probably under the direction of Godwin, Earl of Wessex and premier Earl of England, it may well have been constructed on the foundations of a much earlier building. Disused through the late nineteenth century the chapel entirely escaped the ravages of Victorian 'restoration' and its wall paintings, only discovered in 1864, have been described as the most important series in a Hampshire church apart from Winchester. In particular the narrative mural on the north wall of the chancel is unusual for its completeness and quality.

IDSWORTH to OLD WINCHESTER HILL

Autumn in the beech woods and hangers of the Queen Elizabeth Country Park. The park, the largest in Hampshire and straddling the A3 trunk road, contains some 560 hectares of wood and downland and with its many footpaths, tracks and trails gives easy access to the hills and adjacent South Downs Way.

As the South Downs sweep into Hampshire, the character of the countryside starts to change once again. Beyond Butser Hill the land takes on a lower, more cultivated and undulating form of rolling fields and small woodlands. As far as the Meon Valley, the proposed National Park boundary, encompassing the East Hampshire Area of Outstanding Natural Beauty, stretches north in a series of convoluting curves and shapes almost to the town of Alton. In the more remote and empty parts of this land-scape, it is difficult to believe that it forms the hinterland of one of the most densely populated areas of Europe – the City of Portsmouth.

THE
BAT & BALL

Cricket at Hambledon. Once a market town in the Middle Ages but now a large village, Hambledon became the first major centre in the country for serious cricket with its Cricket Club playing on nearby Broadhalfpenny Down since the eighteenth century. Cricket's early history seems particularly associated with the Downs of Southern England and records exist of a form of the game played by pupils of Winchester College in the 1640s. No doubt other variations of the game were played on different grounds as well but it is the name of Hambledon that has an essential place in the game's pioneering years with the present day rules being laid down by the club in 1774. This sign outside the Bat & Ball public house overlooking Broadhalfpenny Down gives a clear indication of cricket in its formative days.

The view from near the summit of the grassy Butser Hill looking towards the village of East Meon in the soft light of a late spring evening. At 270m the hill is the highest on the main South Downs ridge. Charles Dickens in his *Nicholas Nickleby* described the hill and its surroundings as 'a height so steep as to hardly be accessible to any but the sheep and goats that fed upon its sides'. The hill is a superb viewpoint from which on a clear day one can see some 65km to the spire of Salisbury Cathedral.

Court House, East Meon. East Meon was a manor of the bishops of Winchester from before the Norman Conquest and Court House was the Manor House, its name being derived from the manorial courts held here. The principal part of the present building was built in 1396 when William of Wykeham was bishop. It consists of a shortened great hall, buttery and pantry on the ground floor with a great chamber and closet above. The great hall at its south end was built on to a chapel but this, with a south wing, was demolished in the fifteenth century. However, what is left is a remarkably untouched example of a medieval manor house with a timber and brick farmhouse wing later added. After long years of neglect, the house was purchased in 1927 by the architect Morley Horder who carried out restorations, adding a north wing and laying out the beautiful gardens. The village of East Meon is often regarded as Hampshire's loveliest village.

The black Tournai marble font in the Norman church of All Saints at East Meon is undoubtedly the church's greatest treasure. Made by the famous sculptors of Tournai in Flanders the font was brought from Belgium to the church around 1150 down the Scheldt river, across the North Sea and English Channel and then overland to East Meon. It was almost certainly a gift from the bishop of Winchester, Henry of Blois, who as Lord of the Manor was described by a contemporary observer as 'being most earnest in the beautifying of churches'. There are four examples of such fonts in Hampshire, three others in England, some fifty in Belgium and Northern France and two in Germany. Most are covered in richly carved Romanesque style ornamental designs, often of symbolic meaning and the East Meon example tells the story of Adam and Eve. The photograph shows part of the west face depicting a flat earth supported on pillars and arches and surmounted by mythical beasts combining the elements of mammals, fish, birds and reptiles. All Saints church itself was built on a grand scale from about 1080 to 1150 and has been described by Pevsner as one of the most thrilling village churches in Hampshire.

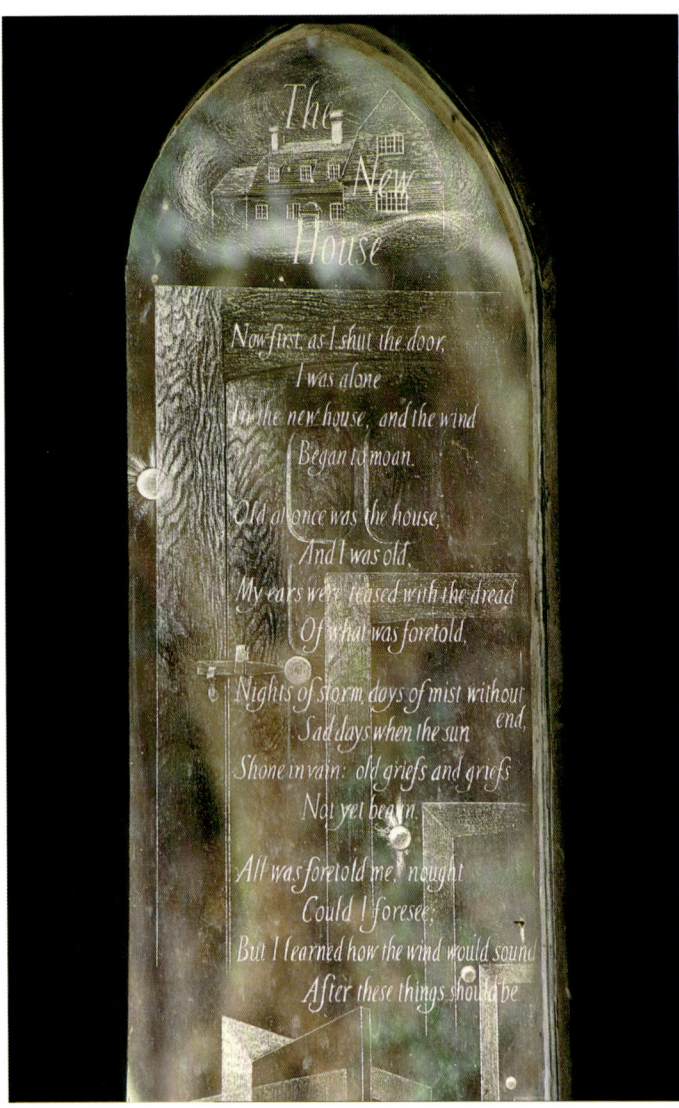

Within the church of All Saints at Steep near Petersfield are two small windows in the south wall that celebrate the life of the poet Edward Thomas who lived nearby and was killed at the Battle of Arras in 1917. These memorial windows were designed and engraved by Lawrence Whistler in 1978 to mark the centenary of the poet's birth. Initially a literary critic and nature writer, Thomas started to write poetry in 1913, encouraged by Robert Frost; he will always be remembered as one of the War Poets and for his beautiful evocation of the English landscape. The window shown here is engraved with illustrations and words of one of his poems *The New House*, the house itself on a hilltop among the beech hangers above Steep overlooking the Downs and where Thomas and his family were first occupants. Another of his poems *The Lane* reflects his interest in the local scene and the darkening shadow of his war experiences:

Some day, I think there will be people enough
In Froxfield to pick all the blackberries
Out of the hedges of Green Lane, the straight
Broad lane where now September hides herself
in bracken and blackberry, harebell and dwarf gorse.

Another evocation of the countryside, wild flowers on the South Downs. The richness of plant species varies considerably depending on soil, elevation and exposure to sunshine. The often short, dense turf and chalk grassland can contain numerous flowers and herbs, changing the predominant colours of the sward as the seasons progress and which in turn support the many varieties of butterflies, insects and bird life to be found.

Decorative terracotta tiled panels, Massey's Folly, Farringdon. The combined village hall and school at Farringdon was begun in 1870 being designed and built by the Rev. Thomas Massey helped by a labourer and carpenter and completed some thirty years later. Known as Massey's Folly, the highly flamboyant, bizarre, colourful and substantial building with its two towers was constructed simply because of his urge to build, often being re-designed in the process. On completion it also featured some seventeen bedrooms and in more recent times has become one of the subjects of television's 'restoration' programmes. Massey died in 1939 having been rector for sixty-two years.

Colour in the Hampshire countryside. A glorious early summer's day near East Tisted.

The church of the Holy Trinity at Privett still stands as a local landmark, its tall tower and spire being a commanding feature of the deeply rural surrounding countryside. Designed by the well-known Victorian architect Sir Arthur Blomfield and paid for by Sir William Nicholson of Basing Park the church was completed in 1878, its total height being some 50 metres and featuring a substantial and highly decorative interior. The building is now in the care of the Churches Conservation Trust and a door key can be obtained nearby.

A busy scene at Medstead & Four Marks station on the preserved Mid Hants Railway 'Watercress Line'. The railway was opened in 1865 by the London & South Western Railway Company and ran between Alton and Winchester via Alresford. With its steep gradients it soon became known by enginemen as 'going over the Alps' and the station at Medstead & Four Marks is now the highest in Southern England at almost 200m above sea level. Train services were withdrawn by British Railways in 1973 but the line was reopened between Alresford and Ropley by the Mid Hants Railway Preservation Society in 1977, later extending to Medstead in 1983 and on to Alton in 1985. As one of the country's leading 'heritage' railways the line has become an extremely popular visitor destination and is often used for filming and television purposes. Most trains are steam hauled and during each year several major special events are held including the 'War on the Line' re-enactment weekend when this photograph was taken.

Gilbert White memorial window, Selborne. The stained glass in the south aisle window of the Norman Church of St Mary at Selborne was installed in 1920 as a bicentennial memorial of the birth of the naturalist Gilbert White who lived in the village. It depicts the legend of St Francis preaching to the birds, all of which are mentioned by Gilbert White in his *Natural History and Antiquities of Selborne,* first published in 1789. In the background can be seen the church, the great yew tree of some 1400 years old (sadly blown down in 1990) and the vicarage where White was born. As the home of White, England's first ecologist, the village has become world famous and the house where he spent most of his life called 'The Wakes' is now a museum. Restored internally to its eighteenth-century appearance and furnishings and with its gardens presented as White described, the museum now receives thousands of visitors each year. Gilbert White died in 1793 but the interest in his *Natural History of Selborne* has never diminished and it remains one of the most popular books ever published. White was particularly fond of the steep beech-clad hillside above the village and both the zig-zag path up which he climbed and Selborne hanger itself are now protected by the National Trust.

Lavender fields between Selborne and Alton. These fields provide a colourful scene in early summer when the flowers are harvested for herbal and perfumery purposes. Further such crops can be found at Lordington near Chichester.

A simple wreath from the Aldershot Branch of the Normandy Veterans Association decorates the plain gravestone of Field Marshall Bernard Law, 1st Viscount Montgomery of Alamein who died in 1976. He is buried at the church of the Holy Cross at Binsted near Alton and as one of the most famous of all wartime leaders, his grave is still visited by many old colleagues and military service personnel for a few quiet moments of reflection.

Late afternoon on Old Winchester Hill. Above the steep west- and south-facing slopes overlooking the Meon Valley lies the prominent Iron Age hillfort of Old Winchester Hill constructed on a projecting spur of the Downs and dating back some 2500 years. Within its ramparts on the crest of the hill are the remains of Bronze Age burial mounds possibly built a further 2000 years before. It is thought that the fort acted as a defended settlement for a Celtic chieftain and with its wide-ranging views has been enjoyed by generations of Hampshire people ever since. The fort is now incorporated into the Old Winchester Hill National Nature Reserve where numerous footpaths take in the steep slopes, adjoining woodland and high-level viewpoints. The varied topography provides an interesting diversity of chalk downland habitat for many wild plants, insects, animals and bird life. Amongst the specialities to be found on the reserve are several species of orchids, numerous cowslips, ox-eye daisy, juniper and Chalkhill Blue butterflies.

The view looking east from Beacon Hill back towards the Meon Valley. The River Meon rises as a classic chalk stream from a downland spring near East Meon and the river's wide green valley has become famous for its string of attractive villages, many with churches dating back to Saxon times. The names of East and West Meon, Brockbridge, Corhampton, Droxford, Exton, Meonstoke, Soberton and Warnford have become Hampshire household words and quite literally a world apart from the City of Portsmouth near the river's mouth. Beacon Hill is also a National Nature Reserve and noted for the thirteen species of wild orchids that can be found here.

THE MEON VALLEY to WINCHESTER

Saxon sundial, Corhampton church. Situated on the south wall of this simple undedicated church the sundial (with its leaf decoration) is divided into eight 'tides' rather than twelve hours. The dial is carved from a stone quite different from any other stone in the church and possible pre-dates the building itself that is thought to have been built about 1020.

From the Meon Valley onwards, the area of the proposed South Downs National Park starts to shrink, hemmed in by the River Itchen to the north and the steadily encroaching presence of the Southampton connurbation to the south. The Downs themselves continue to lose height with wider, more open, spacious fields and isolated clumps of trees. The emphasis here is very much on cultivation rather than classic short cropped turf. At 176m Cheesefoot Head marks the western outcrop of these hills as the ground falls away finally to the City of Winchester.

West Meon has become a village sought by cricket enthusiasts for its association with Thomas Lord who is buried in the churchyard of St John Evangelist. As first owner, Thomas Lord founded the famous Lords Cricket Ground at St John's Wood, London in 1787 and the shadows behind his grave, shown here, give a ghostly impression of a cricket team standing around in reverence. The church itself was rebuilt by the young architect George Gilbert Scott, later famous for many great Victorian buildings and monuments, and is notable for the outstanding quality of its beautiful knapped flint walling.

A busy summer's afternoon at West Meon village Fête held in the grounds of West Meon House. Blue skies, a lovely garden, cups of tea, scones and jam, a small brass band, book, plant and bric-a-brac stalls – for many a perfect day out.

This page and opposite: Meon Valley village scenes at Corhampton, Droxford, Exton, Meonstoke, Warnford and West Meon showing the nature of many of the attractive domestic buildings to be found. *Above:* The church of St Andrew, Meonstoke with its attractive Welsh-style tower and cap.

Above: The church of Our Lady, Warnford, with its magnificent Norman tower, built in the spacious grounds of Warnford Park.

Bottom left: Droxford's church of St Mary and All Saints featuring work and architectural styles from the Norman period right through until the nineteenth century.

Village tapestry. Within the parish church of St Simon and St Jude in the village of Bramdean hangs this illustrative tapestry featuring many of the local buildings and places of interest. The portion of the tapestry shown in the photograph includes the church, war memorial, Bramdean House and Manor and the prominent copper beech trees that line several of the roads in the area. The tapestry was woven between 1992 and 1998 by many of the local villagers.

The Gypsy Church, Bramdean Common. A brick paved path leads to this minute corrugated iron church situated in dense woodland on the edge of Bramdean Common. Built in 1883 to serve the gypsies who once lived there, the building is painted bright green and white and complete with a single bell turret. Behind the church a tiny graveyard just a few metres square has been laid out amongst the trees, a simple, moving haven of peace.

Hinton Ampner House. Situated high on a hill with magnificent views over parkland and the rolling Hampshire countryside, the neo-Georgian house to be seen today was built in 1937 (and later partly rebuilt after a fire in 1960), only the cellar remaining from the original building of about 1800. Surrounding the house, the 5-hectare gardens have been described as a masterpiece of design and one of the great gardens of the twentieth century. Laid out by Ralph Dutton, 8th and last Lord Sherborne, the gardens combine formal layouts with informal planting in numerous colours and shades. The property and gardens are now in the care of the National Trust, the house containing a fine collection of Ralph Dutton's regency furniture and paintings.

RECTION OF THEIR BODIES &IN Y MERITS &MERCY OF
ALONE SAVIOVR, TO BE PARTAKERS OF Y COMFORTA
COME YE BLESSED & RECEIVE Y KINGDOME PREPA
A GOOD LIFE HATH Y DAYES NVMBRED, EC[?]
BVT A GOOD NAME ENDVRETH FOR EVER[?]

Tichborne family monument, St Andrew's church, Tichborne. The part Norman church of St Andrew features an interesting and unusual interior. Within the building is a separate dedicated chapel for the Tichborne family with monuments dating back to 1619. The family who have owned lands in the village since the early twelfth century have remained true to the Roman Catholic faith despite the Reformation and their chapel separated by iron railings from the remainder of the church is almost unique. St Andrew's is one of only three churches in the entire country to have continued to provide a place of worship for both Anglican and Roman Catholic faiths down the centuries.

Harvest window, Tichborne. The church of St Andrew also includes four beautifully coloured celebratory windows depicting the four agricultural church festivals of plough, rogation, lammas and harvest. The windows were renewed to mark the 2000 Millennium and funded by public subscription. They were made by the Salisbury Cathedral Workshops, the designs being based on local views around the village. Tichborne is also well known for the famous Tichborne Claimant law case of 1871 and for the tradition of the Tichborne Dole when flour is distributed to the villagers each year, a custom started by Roger de Tichborne in 1150.

Fields of linseed provide a colourful summer variation to the Hampshire landscape near Gander Down. This scene gives a good indication of the low, wide-open downland to be found in this area, in places forming a simple rolling plateau.

For many the River Itchen at Ovington is one of the most beautiful parts of East Hampshire. Flowing from its source near Cheriton, the river almost defines the northern boundary of the proposed South Downs National Park on its independent journey to Winchester and ultimately the sea. Nearby the river is joined by the smaller Alre and Candover streams and the waters here have become famous for their watercress beds, outstanding clarity and trout fishing. A walk alongside the river and its associated water meadows on a fine summer's day from Ovington to Itchen Stoke can be a treat to the senses.

Georgian church interior, Avington. The church of St Mary at Avington is regarded as having one of the finest unspoilt Georgian interiors in the country. Built of brick, the church is situated back from the road and forms part of the boundary walling to Avington Park Estate, once owned by the 3rd Duke of Chandos. Designed by an unknown architect, the church was built for the Duke's wife between 1768 - 71. Within, the hardwood box pews are carefully graded in size according to the status of their occupants, the Squire's pew for use by the big house, being the largest and most ornate with an adjacent separate exterior entrance. A three-decker pulpit, desks for clerk and reader, a Venetian east window, a small music gallery and an elegant colour scheme complete this harmonious scene. Nearby the River Itchen fans out to make a lake behind the imposing Avington House which dates from the late sixteenth century and is now converted into luxury flats and apartments.

Hampshire 'bun' cottage, Beauworth. Described as a one-and-a-half storeyed building, the typical Hampshire 'bun' cottage with its thatched roof stretching down over shallow upper floor windows and often featuring thatched half-hipped ends is probably the most commonly found older style of rural cottage in the county. Walling materials are generally brick or flint but occasionally stone depending on the cottage's location.

Light and shadow across Ovington Down looking south near Cheesefoot Head. William Cobbett once said of this area, 'There are not many finer spots in England ….. here are hill, dell, water, meadow, woods, cornfields, downs: and all of them very fine and beautifully disposed….. I like nothing more than a country where high downs prevail, with here and there a large wood on the top or side of a hill, and where you see, in the deep dells, here and there a farmhouse, and here or there a village, the buildings sheltered by a group of lofty trees'.

Cheesefoot Head. The South Downs reach their western climax at Cheesefoot Head after which the hills steadily drop away to the City of Winchester. The Head, with Great Clump behind offers long panoramic views to both south and west. Immediately below, the vast natural amphitheatre – sometimes used for special outdoor events – was the site where General Eisenhower addressed the Allied forces before the 1944 D-Day landings.

Shadows of history, the Roman city walls of Winchester. The history of Winchester is the history of England. Recognised by the early Celtic tribes followed by the Belgae, the Romans and the Saxons as an important site, being close to the Downs and a crossing point of the River Itchen, Winchester became the capital of Wessex and the country's capital after unification of England in the ninth century. King Egburt was crowned here in 829 and by the time of King Alfred (871-901) the city had become a centre of great learning. Using the Roman defences as a framework, Alfred created the street pattern that still survives today. William the Conqueror kept Winchester as his capital and even by the late twelfth and thirteenth centuries when most government functions had moved to London, Parliament still continued to meet here on occasions, the city retaining much of its earlier importance and being known as the 'old capital'. Charles II almost brought the Government back to Winchester as late as the seventeenth century with a planned Royal Palace on its outskirts. Architecturally the city is one of the richest in the country with buildings of every period after the thirteenth century and famous of course, for its magnificent Norman Cathedral. With its numerous historic streets and alleyways, riverside walks and gardens, the city has now become a leading tourist destination and a fitting culmination of this photographic journey across the South Downs from Eastbourne.

Winchester, the Hospital of St Cross. Situated on the banks of the River Itchen and surrounded by meadows, woodland and the sound of running water, the Hospital of St Cross lies only about 3 km south-east of the city centre. Founded by Bishop Henry de Blois in 1136 to house 'thirteen poor men and to feed one hundred local people daily', it has been described as England's oldest and most perfect almshouse. The buildings generally, including the lodgings, are grouped around two sides of a quadrangle and mostly now date back to the fifteenth and sixteenth centuries. The adjacent church of St Cross almost closing the quadrangle has a cathedral-like quality in its Norman construction with typical rounded windows, massive piers and lofty vaulted ceilings. Still true to its founder's original aims, the hospital offers the Wayfarers Dole of a morsel of bread and horn of beer to present day visitors.

King Arthur's Table. Little remains of William the Conqueror's castle in Winchester since it was demolished by Parliament during the Civil War but the adjacent Great Hall, built between 1222 and 1236 by Henry III still survives. Regarded as the finest medieval hall in England, after Westminster Hall, it was once the centre of court and government life but the magnificent building still houses the representation of the legendary Round Table of King Arthur's knights. The 6m diameter table is thought to have been constructed during the late thirteenth century, originally undecorated, but later painted to feature King Arthur himself, a central Tudor Rose and places marked out and inscribed for 24 named knights. The table weighs almost two tonnes and is made from 121 pieces of oak.

Medieval floor tiles, Winchester Cathedral. Acclaimed as one of the world's great buildings, Winchester Cathedral is the longest cathedral in Europe. The cathedral was begun under the orders of William the Conqueror in 1079, partly covering the site of an earlier Saxon church built by King Alfred, and completed in 1404. Featuring several architectural styles from the Norman transepts to the rebuilt soaring Perpendicular nave, the building dominates internally by sheer size alone, seemingly stretching to infinity over its great length. Within are seven carved chantry chapels and numerous tombs, mortuary chests and memorials to the many ancient kings, bishops, statesmen and writers buried here. The cathedral contains the largest surviving carpet of medieval floor tiles (shown here) in England, the twelfth century Winchester Bible, outstanding works of art and many fine examples of modern glass in its windows, much of the original stained glass having been destroyed during the Reformation. At the beginning of the twentieth century the cathedral was in real danger of collapse, due to the rising of the surrounding water table causing rot and disintegration of the building's original timber foundations. This was prevented mainly due to the skill and courage of William Walker a deep sea diver who spent six years underpinning the walls with concrete. He was awarded the Royal Victorian Medal by George V and is immortalised by a brass statue in the cathedral.

Light and stone. Part of the south transept and Perpendicular-styled nave of Winchester Cathedral.

This photographic journey commenced at Eastbourne on the Sussex coast simply because the South Downs seem associated in peoples' minds with the county of Sussex rather than Hampshire. Every year countless walkers and riders undertake the same journey, probably using the South Downs Way and starting at either end of this magnificent chain of hills. In the east possibly the most elegant of seaside resorts and in the west, as has just been described, the outstanding historic interest of Winchester. Both directions have their merits but it is of course the countryside in between that is the real attraction – one of the few remaining areas in Southern England where real peace, quiet isolation and emptiness can still be enjoyed and where the song of the skylark is an almost constant companion. Here in this rolling landscape with its great open skies and innumerable moods of light, shadow and colour is the very essence of England – something that should be precious to us all.

ACKNOWLEDGEMENTS

Once again I would like to thank the many people who have helped me in the compilation of this book by allowing photography, providing information and for advising on or contributing to captions and text. I am therefore most grateful to the following:

Mr and Mrs G. Bartlett (Court House, East Meon); Mr P. Jerome (Petworth Cottage Museum); Miss S. Philip (Charleston Trust); Miss K. Simms; the Management and Staff at the Amberley Working Museum; Bignor Roman Villa; the Cass Sculpture Foundation; the Churches Conservation Trust; the Firle Estate; the Hollycombe Steam Collection; the National Trust and the Weald & Downland Open Air Museum.

In particular I wish to thank Joy once more for her infinite patience, support and hard work in typing the manuscript and overcoming a reluctant computer. Finally, of course, to Steven Pugsley and his enthusiastic colleagues at Halsgrove for all their assistance.

My late father was tremendously fond of the South Downs and knew parts of them well, particularly in East Sussex. His ashes are now scattered there but his company was with me many times as I explored this unique and much loved range of hills.

REFERENCE SOURCES

There are numerous books, booklets, papers, leaflets and guides about the South Downs. It is an impossible task to mention them all but the following have been invaluable as reference sources:

Arscott, D. *Curiosities of West Sussex* SB Publications, 1993

AA *Illustrated Guide to Britain* Drive Publications, 1974

AA/Ordnance Survey *Leisure Guide, Hampshire and the Isle of Wight* AA Publishing, 1996

AA/Ordnance Survey *Leisure Guide, South Downs* AA/Ordnance Survey Publishing, 1988

Brabbs, D. *Abbeys and Monasteries* Weidenfeld & Nicholson, 1999

Brandon, P. *Sussex* Robert Hale, 2006

Brandon, P. *The South Downs* Phillimore, 1998

Brandon, P. *The Sussex Landscape* Hodder & Stoughton, 1974

Boogaart, P. *A272* Pallas Athene, 2000

George, M. *The South Downs* Pavilion, 1992

Hadfield, J. *The Shell Guide to England* Michael Joseph, 1970

Jenkins, S. *England's Thousand Best Churches* Penguin Books, 1999

Lesley, K. and Short, B. *An Historical Atlas of Sussex* Phillimore, 1999

Lloyd, D. *Historic Towns of Kent and Sussex* Victor Gollancz, 1991

Mason, P. and Harrison, J. *Hampshire A Sense of Place* Hampshire Books, 1994

McGowan, I. *A Portrait of Brighton & Hove* Halsgrove, 2004

McGowan, I. *A Portrait of Portsmouth, Gosport & Southsea* Halsgrove, 2005

McGowan, I. *Moods of Sussex* Halsgrove, 2006

Mee, A. *The Kings England: Sussex* Hodder & Stoughton, 1964

Millmore, P. *South Downs Way: National Trail Guides* Aurum Press, 2004

Mitchell, W. *East Sussex – A Shell guide* Faber & Faber, 1978

Pailthorpe, R. and McGowan, I. *Chichester A Contemporary View* John Wiley, 1994

Pailthorpe, R. and McGowan, I. *Chichester A Millennium View* John Wiley, 2000

Pevsner, N. and Lloyd, D. *The Buildings of England: Hampshire and the Isle of Wight* Yale University Press, 2002

Pevsner, N. and Nairn, I. *The Buildings of England: Sussex* Penguin Books, 1975

Sellman, D. and Arscott, D. *Sussex A Colour Portrait* Countryside Books, 2004

Skinner, D. *Sussex – People and History* Crowood Press, 2002

Swinfen, W. and Arscott, D. *Hidden Sussex* BBC Radio Sussex, 1984

Talbot, R. and Whiteman, R. *The Garden of England* Weidenfeld & Nicholson, 1995

Thomas, E. *Collected Poems* Faber and Faber, 1974

Wales, T. *The West Sussex Village Book* Countryside Books, 1984

White, G. *The Natural History and Antiquities of Selborne* Dent, 1971

Guides and leaflets to the many attractions, museums, places of interest and churches featured within this book.